BASED ON ACTUAL EVENTS

Based
on Actual Events

ROBERT MOORE

THE POETRY IMPRINT AT VÉHICULE PRESS

Published with the generous assistance of The Canada Council for the
Arts and the Canada Book Fund of the Department of Canadian Heritage,
Government of Canada.

Funded by the Government of Canada
Financé par le gouvernement du Canada |  Canadä

SIGNAL EDITIONS EDITOR: CARMINE STARNINO

Cover design: David Drummond
Photo of the author: Judith Mackin
Set in Filosofia and Minion by Simon Garamond
Printed by Marquis Book Printing Inc.

Dépôt légal, Library and Archives Canada and the
Bibliothèque national du Québec, third trimester 2016.

LIBRARY AND ARCHIVES CANADA CATALOGUING IN PUBLICATION

Moore, Robert John, 1950-, author
Based on actual events / Robert Moore.

Poems.
Issued in print and electronic formats.
ISBN 978-1-55065-455-4 (paperback). – ISBN 978-1-55065-461-5 (epub)

I. Title.

PS8576.061525B38 2016   C811'.6   C2016-902052-5
C2016-902053-3

Published by Véhicule Press, Montréal, Québec, Canada
www.vehiculepress.com

Distribution in Canada by LitDistCo
www.litdistco.ca

Distributed in the U.S. by Independent Publishers Group
www.ipgbook.com

Printed in Canada on FSC certified paper.

The confusing signals, the impurity of the signal, gives you verisimilitude, as when you attend a funeral and notice that it's being poorly done.

DONALD BARTHELME

1

Ever since beauty went futile
poets write for other poets;
serial killers, mailing each other clues.
Drink only to reveal the ship the bottle harbours.
Rigging perverse as a multiplex.

A study by critics, taking cautious turns
at the Heresy of Paraphrase Follies,
writes the poem. An original
Netflix series rolls over in its sleep
and suffocates the entire harvest.

In a culture of image and simulacra
the poets offer to sharpen your scissors
and knives so you can cut your losses
from last week's flyer. Your indifference
raises a welt but demures on the scar.

Oh brave, direct, unforgettable voice,
we waited for you to put it into words.
Even in the hands of a modern master, our series
of *cris de sang* is the sleeve tattoo
everyone lives to regret.

2

Today we ventured forth, a realist in fabulist clothing. Everywhere
we went we passed off the green carnations of the improbable as
the white lilies of the inevitable. No one who is not something
of a fool saw us coming, for where we live chance is a form
of authorial control. What struck us most was how thick
ennui lay upon the environs. We felt it underfoot,
vague as rotting snow. Or time. And then it hit us in a series
of throbs: Buying anything with a lifetime warranty
is what passes these days for prayer.

3

We spent the day's diminishing woof imagining your conversation
with yourself. Something singular swam between
the lines. A shape. A dark, suggestive shape.

Turns out it was one of the Brontës, her current take
on the family umlat two juggler's balls. Not much
of a trick. Depends on the juggler, sobbed the juggler.
Nipples like pissholes in the permafrost,
is how one inflamed reader. None of this is helping.

The depression left by the nineteenth century
goes with everything we own. And now
you're no longer with us, our modesty seems contrived;
undressing yet another object lesson in the limits
of The Object Lesson. The sibilance of fabric against flesh
merely one of the names you go by. One of far too many,
if you take our meaning.

4

Every Theory of Everything has a dirty little secret.
If you listen very closely, you can hear it ticking.
A doll's heartbeat. One of those dolls that comes to life
when no one's looking and heads straight for the cutlery drawer.
The glass eyes of our T of E look right through you. Its gaze is pitiless.
You are as nothing before it, merely an excrescence in cheap shoes;
a collocation of vanities, clueless when it comes to divining
the laws of the genre that create and contain you. Until
it's too late. That, however, is not its secret. Well,
not anymore.

5

Ironists are less likely to get cancer
but more likely to be struck by lightning.
If you find that sobering, you're not drinking enough.

Qualifying as an ironist isn't difficult. You can wear
what you like to the meetings and eat what you want
afterwards. Mincemeat a popular choice. No ironist
worthy of the distinction can ever go the movies alone.

Shortly before his death, David Foster Wallace revised
his views on irony. News that he'd adjusted course
tore through the fleet. The loss with all hands of *The Relative*
in the action that followed briefly put things back into perspective.

At their executions, ironists refuse the blindfold
but never the last cigarette. Several have used the occasion
to take up chain smoking. At the last moment, the ironist
will yell "Viva…!," the ellipsis brief in the air,
vivid as bullet holes in the possibilities.

6

We despair the relative worth of our despair.
Low grade despair is normal, high grade a national
shame. We turn our televisions off and on, not deigning
to have our dreams besmirched. We assume an attitude
of studied indifference, which burns about eleven calories a minute.
We don't care who is on whose yard line or how many shoulder-
launched rockets or kroners. That is, we pretend not to care.
Fact is, we care. Between our pretense and our actual care
is a significant gap in which certain life forms marshal effort.
Likely denizens include dust mites. We feel about dust mites
pace the usual abstract fashion, sort of how you must feel about
Harrison Ford. We once saw Harrison Ford coming out
of a restaurant in Paris so of course it's not the same
for us. Remember that part in *Raiders of the Lost Ark*
when the Nazis crack open the ark? Someone
should really bottle that feeling.

7

Been left of late bereft of sufficient affect? Blame the word-hoard.
It's a phrase you're going through. I too dislike it, especially lyric's warp;
the roaring silence, the headlong pause. All that natural detail
boasts nothing on the other side. For the history of grief,
an empty wallet and a handkerchief. *Honeymoon* is a dead
metaphor and therefore mucho. Hemingway,
challenged to come up with the shortest story ever, overshot
by six words. When Hemingway killed himself he overshot
his sense of himself as princely. Bull's-eyed the entire universe
with a single breathe and squeeze. *Princely* is not a word
in Papa's hoard. Note the present tense.
Which explains *nada.*

8

We esteem poems that regard the page as a total failure of nerve.
That come with no guarantees but a generous return policy.
That got the game granular. Jitterbug at the end of the driveway
in loose shirts just daring life to throw the book at them.
Admit it: your poems would rather be out pissing ether,
getting lost in themselves, etc. The best poems start out as follows:
"So we were out ice fishing with Kafka when suddenly…."
Some openings you never get past.

9

The spiked heads of our enemies at the city gates
encouraged to gibber without constraint on any subject
under the sun. Rain or shine. The latest lip reading app
automatically downloaded to everyone's smart phone.
Our views on free speech the envy of the civilized world.

10

So we reverse-engineered the awesome and all we got
was this lousy poesy: Apollo, on awful bender of space/time,
delivers Icarus by daffodil sweet heels. One slap is all, and
backwashed through a film of borrowed green, green as thought,
breaching an urn of spermicidal foam, and he's off,
piloting the first manned mission to Mars. Ploughman,
it's not the fall that kills, even from a jocund view of self as
whole, tricked out in the pulse of immortal longing. For how
giving the earth, unforgiving the ground. And how
deadly the heavens must certain prove, tribe to tribe, age to age.
Every sprinkle of stars, those spots of time, seeds of a plot against us.
Antigone, that cold fish, for whom every word invoked
every other word in every possible combination
couldn't do small talk to save her life. The dogs
brought back from space never spoke again.
The monkeys couldn't stop screaming.

We have yet to be invited to any of our author photos. In one
they're at a school dance, fussing over the yearbook's scheme
of vanishing points. They've established a perimeter. Music
peels from the rafters. Stalagmites of grey substance abound.

In this one, you'll note, we're killing time like nobody's business.
And here we're looking down, a moon weighing numbers
from last year's body count.

Write enough books and you become a somebody.
Try it. You'll see. And if not, there are always compensations.
Such as happy hour. Say what you will, faces don't amount to much.
Truth is, they never did. Under the covers, learning skull-
duggery.

12

Mother dropped this world like a bad habit, addressing
her cancer formally via The Information Age. Thus
did it prosper, opening a marble office in her exhaustion.

Her provinces shrunk under a chemical sun; months
an arabesque of veins, decaying afternoons and coffee scum.
The obituary arrived in a bad suit, a patchwork of ampersands.

A young woman in a snapshot, bathed in that moment's radiation.
Her bare legs never more final or absolute. We still have the rest
of her objective correlatives around here someplace.

Just give us a minute.

13

John Wayne bit the dust in seven of his 162 films. That's
a mortality rate of 4.32%. Pretending to be someone
else is not without its risks. Sniper fire alone
accounted for 28.57% of his deaths. He just didn't
see it coming. None of his film deaths
was from cancer, which makes sense. His last words
were 'That's a wrap!" When John Wayne died
most of the dads in our neighbourhood decided
to carry on without him. Most, but not all.
Two or three saddled up and headed west.
Their wives stood framed in their doorways
as the music swelled and the credits rolled, waving
the way you wave when you know the person you're waving to
won't ever look back, not ever, and the soft whir
of the Panaflex in the parlour is now your only comfort.
But because the only death you'll ever know in this life
is someone else's, no dads saddled up and headed west
and their wives were spared the doorway. In our exit survey,
in response to the statement "Real life isn't a movie,"
only 4.32% of respondents chose "Strongly agree."

14

Life is interesting for the way it combines proximity and distance.
So is Winnipeg. And quartz. The unreliability of language

one of the enduring wonders of the world. Arguably its only
enduring wonder. Our disappointment balanced against our hope,
the way shadows sing of the sun they'll never share. And yet,

mouths opens. *I love you* hasn't worn out its welcome. A standard
exercise in creative writing classes is to demand the inclusion
of three otherwise unrelated objects, such as a comb, a fish
and dialectical materialism. Everyone gets the hang of it.

15

We arrive to answer the charges. As is our right, we ask
they be read slowly. And with feeling. Everyone
duly informed that stones larger than your own fist
require a special carrying permit. And that the crew
from *America's Funniest Home Videos* is due
on site any minute, so best be husbanding the ammo.

When the jury retires, there are twelve less souls to worry about.
They ask to review photos of the crime scene. The judge
admonishes them for lack of imagination. Then they ask
for the lyrics to Leonard Cohen's *Closing Time.*
Then it's a piece of the true cross. Then
another word for "discandy."

When the jury returns, the beards on the women
create a minor flap. The defense moves for a mistrial.
We all go out for tapas and dance our asses off.

16

As a rhetorical strategy, the first-person use of *we*
has a storied history. Wayne Gretzky occasionally and
the Queen (secretly drafted by the Leafs in 1963 as a form
of public art) invariably. The first person to use it
was Henry II in 1169. He did it to remind the assembled—
so given to disremember—that when *we* speak, God's lips move.
The eyes of the nobles first treated to *pluralis majestatis*
kept rolling heavenward. Among his mortal enemies, old Henry,
if asked, would have numbered three of his eight children.
In response to the question, "Before a game, do you
have any special rituals of preparation?" Gretzky replied,
"We like to put baby powder on the end of our sticks."
True story.

17

We loot world religions for low hanging fruit.
At night, in the desert, we sound trumpets of horn
then wait to see what the se'irim drag in. The results?
Totally awesome.

Folks assume we have no conception of a higher being,
of something above and sublimely beyond. Nothing
could be further from the truth. Every find
vellicates the ventricles of our conviction.

We hold services on Tuesdays. We take turns shouting out
responses to Plate 6 from our signed eighth edition of
Mutus Liber. The first one to keep a straight face
has to rearrange the geegaws in the ice house
into some kind of disorder.

Sunday with only his image to steer by, Adam—
inveterate hobbyist—fashioned yet another god from clay,
the third that day, but something in the way
of self nursed from emptiness. The original ceramist
overlooking the garden from a complacent window
and his cooling, fresh-wrought, hollow man; the light-sick,
listening to the familiar roar of silence within silence,
the fire-soaked birth of alone. To our perfect present horror
of the found world, the knock with no one there,
of clones. Ineluctably, they come and go, muscling to and fro
birds wild with longing by the blue-green, glassy-eyed
across the ceiling like enraptured Narcissus by the sky-slick pool,
apes brained by warm voices on the dictaphone
nose to nose and fingertip. Thus we address you, Gentle Reader,
whole worlds in whatever mess of detail springs to mind
via verse and verso, here on the ragged, collapsing edge of
let us call them, for lack of better, *nobjects*,
an infinitely unfolding genesis.

19

Turning now to art made for tourists: its purity shames us.
Take this piece, the plastic Eiffel Tower that doubles
as a corkscrew. It's a fine example, a pure example.
Of what is it an example? Why, it's an example of itself.

The heretic Benjamin argued that the masses contribute to the loss
of aura by seeking constantly to bring things closer; they create
reproducible realities and hence destroy uniqueness. But
keep in mind that Benjamin died two years before the birth
of Stephen Hawking and that Arthur C. Clarke had yet
to write anything of consequence. So, in eighty thousand years,
give or take, when aliens on a package tour dig through the ruins
of human civilization and discover it poking through the ash,
this plastic Eiffel Tower corkscrew will truly come into its own.

Under that distant, white, indifferent sun it will whisper uniquely
of the vanished miracles of Châteauneuf-du-Pape, the Latin Quarter,
the year of Our Lord 1889, and erectile dysfunction.

20

Imagine you're wearing a headlamp,
the kind miners wear to get under the earth's skin.
Nicer, of course; a professional mode of tunnel vision.
It's a look that suits you. You be stylin'. Turning your attention
to any subject elevated to a formal procedure. The dignity of work.
Your pizza arrives and the delivery guy, eyes folded
in the throw of your headlamp, confesses he has
these feelings. But what were you expecting?
You turn your head slightly to the left...
and there it is!

21

A good deal of the book, she states in an interview, is,
as they say, 'made up.' At heart, it's about the problem of genre, for
between two genres there exists no natural barrier; that sort
of thinking went out with The Great Chain of Being. To live
is to make fiction, is what she's saying. Okay, good.
That helps. What did she say next? That each work should
aspire to an alchemical, profoundly paratactical commonplace
book desperately in need of its own form? Well, duh. But what
about endings? As a species, we're wired to arrive. Unlike the house cat.
Little Boots, to cite one: the day she died she didn't. (Animals and
literary characters possess no meaningful apprehension of death
even though their grasp of the concept *unintended consequences of one's*
actions is estimable.) Her death and Little Nell's. Cry us a river
if you've heard this one.

22

We keep turning up in other people's dreams. And we know this
how? We're going to get along not famously. Currently,
the house of fame chock full of punters not going through
to the next round. One fine day their lockers emptied,
shields neatly piled on the stoop at the wrong end of the
magno-jector. Only the unfamous truly get the fame thing.
It's like asking a white whale to define *bête noir*. Good luck
with that. Ahab is famous. Melville not so much.
Call us tomorrow. We'll review response strategies.

23

A vanishing twin is a fetus in a multi-gestation pregnancy
which dies in utero and is then reabsorbed by its twin.
Reabsorbed is standard usage in matters this grave.
Absorbed would imply motive. Given the nature of the crime scene,
it is impossible to say how frequently the phenomenon occurs.
The soul of a vanished twin, reluctant to quit the earth,
seeks shelter in mirrors. We think we've seen ours.
It would explain a lot. How else to account for
undertones of hostility in our reflected expression, or
the feeling we're alone even in the warmest company?
When not on duty, a vanished twin pores through
The Complete Book of Baby Names, nursing
its exquisite sense of loss. Perhaps not surprisingly,
following the death of its surviving twin,
the vanished twin soon succumbs
to utter self-absorption.

24

Our dream a density of style, of riddling complexity,
of the greatest possible synchrony with the greatest potential
for accumulated vocable. And since we're sharing, we also like
the phrase "the brain throbbing heart-like" so much we cadged it
from he who borrowed it from she who first fried it up
in the bonedome. Think of it as a species of necromancy
akin to the hypertrophic vintage dice which in
their fuzzy wine-darkedness now scrotalize the streaming wind-
screen of our peregrinations. Next stop? The nearly
absolute impossibility of any of us having arrived here
in the first place. Intimations crack open our chests;
darkness making mouths. Have done! All your life you've lived
in a land where other people die. Generally speaking, the real
is overrated. Except in the mind's eye.
As opposed to that other one.

25

Even under enhanced interrogation the vampire
refused to give us anything. And we tried it all,
shit we didn't even know you could do and still call
yourself human. Nihilo. Zilch. If anything, his smirk
got smirkier, his ass even wiser. And those fangs!
Growing back each time; pellucid as milk,
alert as metal against silk.

So we waited until high noon—both hands reaching for God—
then shoved him out of the van in the Sears parking lot.
It was like you'd lit a gasoline fart. It was like wings
opening inside you.

Over before you could swallow. Seen more ash
at the end of a Virginia Slim. "Holy screaming fuckballs,"
sighed the captain, as much to himself as to the assembled,
we who'd done things we couldn't even share
with ourselves, never mind over breakfast
or lost weekends, in earshot of our televisions,
which knew every lie in the book.

The purpose of the first lover is to make room for the second.
The purpose of the thirteenth is to turn the foregoing twelve into
twenty four eyes embedded in a surface. If they happen
to all blink at once the mechanism instantly breaks down, starts spouting
the kind of scripture you've learned to live without (right there
in the warranty, font the size of everything you ever promised).
The hundredth lover a definite milestone. Her t-shirt states
"Keeping Abreast of Developments." Four inches of Helvetica bold.
Breasts rigid with embarrassment. She takes to calling you 'Buster' in italics.
She'd prefer your sternum pierced. Under her skirt your future yawns.
You can hardly wait.

Love is a sucking chest wound. No,
strike that; too strong; no one's that bitter.
So maybe it feels like a sucking chest wound
to those who haven't had one,
maybe at 2:16 a.m. and baby has just made it
abundantly clear that what you are just isn't enough,
your assets of insufficient mass to generate gravity sufficient
to hold his or her celestial self in orbit around you.
But that feeling passes and love isn't
simply one of the kajillion feelings you have
or had while storming and conniving in its kingdom.
So, what is love? Ah, that my friend, that
is the abiding interest of every poem ever written.
Especially the bad ones, the ones
with sucking chest wounds.

Of Wittgenstein's philosophy it could be said, It's a system
unsystematically arranged. But of what could not the same be said?
The intellectual ferment of pre-1914 Vienna? Glad we cleared that up.
Family on the street we grew up on spoke in tongues.
The son we best remember for an epic fist-fight
disclosed to us one putatively illimitable summer afternoon
that his father "had the gift."
Wittgenstein's mother's name was Leopoldine. Guessing Opa wanted a son.
Bloodied his beak with the first punch.
Our father thought the boy's gifted father a total waste of dermis.
Wittgenstein went to school with Adolf Hitler. Or as A. C. Grayling puts it,
he attended the same school "where his exact contemporary Adolph Hitler
was also a pupil." Whereof we draw our own conclusions.
Our father, angry, spoke in tongues. In a manner of speaking.
Regarding its exact contemporaries, Silence, unfolding its vasty,
laugh-lined wings, would now like a word.

29

Little known fact: Wittgenstein was morbidly obese. We're talking
embonpoint. We're not talking bay window, flap rash the like of which.
Oh yes, the few extant photographs smuggled out of the Weimer
show a maladjusted ectomorph with sensible hair. Another piano case
coffin thus lost to the dead-eyed annals of The Agreed. But really,
isn't this to be expected? How difficult is it to misread a photograph?
Really. Misreading photographs is what we do best. In this one
father steps from the garage with a bottle of vodka
squirreled up his ass. No wait, it's under his arm.
No wait, sorry, our mistake: that's an asp.

Association eats at logic like a newt licking a barn owl
in Twain. Logic, combing its locks, endures. Can't hear *newt*
without conjuring Newton, the lovable adolescent *centaur*
from *The Mighty Hercules*. Those flat-faced afternoons.
Get Herc! he'd cry, anguished by the lack of a vital dimension.
Then the signature summons from his trusty flute.
Then the signature summons from his trusty flute.
Never failed to repeat himself. *Sidekick* a term of art
purloined from pickpocketry. Sidekicks are choric figures
carried in the front pockets of better men.
Is any of this a helping? Once you accept the viability
of the intestinal intrigue subtending the concept 'centaur,'
flute playing inevitable as artillery shells the size of railway cars.
Wide-bodied jets. The fourth of Newton's laws of motion.

31

Lately-cut lawns irresistible to crows fresh
from *The Charterhouse of Parma*, split from black-
veined poplars like phrases, ambling like arthritic museum
guards with gravity's number. A myth, the Stendhal Syndrome.
Even Rilke, that supreme bullshit artist, paintings a grey meringue,
breath in a blender. How many yet do the wooze before Bernini's *St Teresa*?
That marble orgasm. Going down. The clutch at zippo.
(*Blow job* the bastard child of *below job*, so you do the math.)
Bruised brow from where the floor ultimately catches up
like something right out of the seventeenth slash
nineteenth slash twentieth century.

32

When Neil Armstrong died he deserved a twenty-one ray gun
salute. Cousin, whence your japes and gambols? Out vaunting
about? Sometimes when you perch a certain way on the ledge
of the bed, freckled back to us, "Jump!" enters its launch sequence. We confess:
our helmet our pride but not our melting joy. One small step. Beyond,
the moon waits, tonsured by infinity. A species of widowhood. It stopped
tapping one impatient toe during the Copernican Revolution.
Distant progenitor fires the first shot. Spit-take of heavy water.
Love now arrives home from the moon every morning,
complexion ravaged.

33

We haven't yet decided what this next one's about.
Starting now, the implicit may be prized from its shell.
Here, in this, our open source culture; easy as busting a nut.
But that's the whole point, Pilgrim. Otherwise, wherefore
our shared hope to dissolve in topological foam
beneath the Planck length? Where indeed! So let's go amusing
dressed in a smatter of iconographical clues. Nay,
not for us the classic narrative, meathooks spread, palms up vatic
style, parsing the flimsy-whimsy. O, there are days that stand up
inside you! Pray, stay your scroll down yet a little longer. Amnesia
won't take the past away. The trick is to keep piling up observations,
eating the frame. In a fugue state, first thing you do is up
your credit limit. Then double down on the fact that
only seven deck chairs from the original Titantic still exist.

34

Orgy well underway. Too many enfolded to take in. What
a marvelous turnout. Authentic attitude left in other pants. Dick
insists we address him as 'The Hurt.' This again! One of those
fierce, three part microsecond subrosa hissy fits. The worlds
a good set of parentheses compresses to its kisser. We're such
a couple. Definitely the room for a lip-reader.
It's not about filling in gaps so much as their manufacture.
Christ, will you feature those paintings! Fuck me. The temptation
to propose a toast is resistible. We suspend judgment.
Porno on the plasma, cornering the market, teasing us
into thought. We left too much at the door. Like a drunk with a story,
the music too close. And Motorhead. Who disports to Motorhead?
You were expecting maybe Schubert? *Lady in Red*? Now that woman
over there. Those labials recall. There's an odd number of us here.
In various shades. She seems really into it. No, strike that:
she seems. Really. Would she make noises like that if no one
here to hear them? Are we, in fact, speaking through her?
As in a séance? As in the ear of God? As in "down in a hale of money-
shots"? A recording of this would not make a simile-rich environment.
Can one ever do other than watch one's step? We're curiously touched
by Heisenberg's Uncertainty Principle. Our mind's express
of tumefactions. It's nuts this sudden desire to buy something.
Surprising how badly we handle naked; as spectacle, skin isn't a strong
finisher. Happily, as ice-breaker, "Hi there" boasts a half-life
of about two thousand years.

35

Maybe it's time we met. We *all* met, that is. LOL.
A little mixer in the Desert of the Real. Some of you
already acquainted but don't let that micturate all
over your shitkickers. How about you bring the salads?
The point is to avoid hard feelings. Hard feelings
we leave at the hoosegow like shooting iron
in border towns run by progressive marshals.
Speaking of which, let's not invite the dead.
You remember what happened last time, when
Val Kilmer and Doc Holiday got into that dust up, two grow'd men
trying to stuff their shapes into that grass widow's shadow? Why
I can still see Doc slo-mo-ing up behind Val courtesy of an oblique
attenuated as a highwire over the Grand Canyon, the bullet's brisk
exit out the latter's brow trailing tri-coloured ribbons of yonder
like the former was throwing his own little private Arizona.

JPEG actually stands for *Joint Photographic Experts Group*. Are we
boring you? Was actually *actually* necessary? And don't get us started
on The Golden Globes? At the very next Apocalypse Now
everyone involved to be bitch slapped by
Aphrodite for whom *This Time It's Personal*. In a gown
of Trojan tears. A full Brazillian (aka Sphinx) where those
slow thighs come together. Enfolded wedge the size
of the San Andreas Fault. According to Aquinas, every angel
its own species. Makes absolute sense. After all, daguerrotypes
obliged a pinch of mercury vapour. But then, the first use of any new medium
is pornography. Our term for the drive-in theatres now all but vanished
from the outlands? Fingerbowls. Look upon our works ye mighty.
And save any changes.

37

The arresting phrase *wages of sin is death* constitutes
appropriate use of *is*. That's the good news. Bad news is
English has well over 150 euphemisms for the word *vagina*
and not one working euphemism for *euphemism*. No wait,
that *is* the good news. Bad news is *meat curtains*.
Good news is that *meat curtains* is just about as bad
as it gets. Figure concealed behind meat curtains, of course, is
Mr. Death. Only Mr. Death has the *cajones* to stand behind
a jolly set of meat curtains (hands on hips, splayed mitt
bones oddly suggestive of fans a pint-sized stripper might
turn to advantage) waiting to spluge a *boo* at the parting.
Mr. Death speaks only by way of euphemism; it's his métier;
couldn't deliver a straight answer if life depended.
Except one, natch. Whether that's good news or bad news
pretty much depends on your current estimation of the merits
of Peter Pan's remark, "to die will be an awfully great adventure."
While pondering, guests should keep in mind that Peter Pan is probably
the last boy deserving of anyone's confidence on the subject of
meat curtains.

38

Labyrinthine tunnel system connects death and silence.
You think last words, clawing the black lid. You think
mother, pale figure on the lawn at midnight. Mouth ajar, starry-
eyed. Turns out ghosts suck at interior design. Green candles
for ankles lit from within. Like they swallowed the history of metaphor.
Facts wave their empty, simulative sleeves under every streetlamp.
Hitherto underappreciated link between satin-lined coffins and
1993 Christmas Barbie, still in the box. Gussied to the nines. Hitherto
underappreciation definitely where it's at. We prefer to haunt
our own houses, thank you. Confucius say, All meaning gestural.
That said, carriage holding just Emily Dickinson *and* SunSet
Malibu Ken almost certainly a dead end.

39

Nothing easier to violate than syntax. Than a Benedictine's
fundament. Ah, but to what end? The sallied, solid, sullied salad.
Carapace or caul? We're thinking of having our memory pierced.
A platinum dumbbell. Currently the best defense against perish
is a tattoo of the word *tattoo*. Conversely, on the B side, *skin*.
That's putting it out there. For all the world to jangle. But then
the giddy question of font. Ours the golden age of font.
You can't make this shit up.

40

Let us now speak of tweaked commodities and niched markets.
The seamless circuit of production and consumption.
Thus we're bound to ask, When did the constructed subject
of postmodernism become the designed subject of consumerism?
It's a fair question. Now tell us what you're wearing.
The various pressures and textures enwrapping.
We're talking a systematic overestimation of what exists.
Take your time. Relish your investment. Think of Rothko.
As citizens accustomed to life inside purely verbal structures,
survivors describe an oceanic feeling, even those with chronic thalassophobia.
Two firm thumbs to the eyeballs to download the Big Bang trailer.
Meantime, our coffee tables, freighted with trophy text,
crawl the wide littoral between attention and receptivity.

41

You realize, of course, that our method of systematic overinflation
and rhetorical inversion risks lapsing into glib conflation. As when
you touched my cheek. The backs of your fingers brushing. The pale
folds of a mutual hesitation. As when Poggio fetched back Lucretius
from the brink. Not exactly the subtextuality of mnemonic afterimages
pushing toward a pastiche of overt citations, we grant you. And yet.
And yet, the dialectic of reification and reanimation persists.
How is it, darling, that against all reason the more simulacral
our embraces, the moral auratic? Proof of love? In celebration, let's
staple a few kisses to the rectory door. Should we try conjoining
with blinkers off? Yes, yes, we're under construction but
the gift shop remains open for business.

As mode of conveyance we lodge the thought experiment. No,
we're glad you asked! Leatherbound grace notes out by the first post.
As portraiture, we favour the satellite photograph. Today spent driving
a wedge between two degrees of separation: *Gideon's Bible* and
Poe's "The Purloined Letter." Seriously, is the modern motel room's design
primarily a function of memory or desire? Which two parts
of *modern motel room* aren't oxymoronic? On your average motel's bedspread
is the close-packed agglomeration of shot spots under ultraviolet light
the result of a) memory or b) desire? Alien starmaps?
Anthony Perkins and Paris Hilton.

43

In the prolegmenon to The Great Cullings they took only water-
boys. We didn't miss them until a fortnight. No collective recollection
of the last successful intercourse with a swabber. That's when
we divined a motif. Then, as is our wont, we opened yet
another front, mention of which twice made in *Dispatches*.
From directly underneath their ships refuse to take shape;
form a needle in content's haystack. Only from the side.
Only after a liberal dose of rum, the lash, and buggery.
Their science is teaching our circuit boards how to see
Patagonia on a dime. Saviours coalesce into book clubs.
Meantime we few, we happy few, have ordered
a second helping of our whereabouts.

44

We too approve the move to depurated,
fractal rigor. Think Chinese prose, that complex grid
of semantic couplings, aural interlockings, intertextual
allusions, and so forth, and the reader—fully-loaded,
cutis glued to the moment—moves around and
wanders, guided not so much by syntagmatic sequence
as attention to the multiplicity of non-linear textures,
excisions from what normative grammar affords. As in
meeting a stranger. As in drawing breath, only without
the drawing. Or the breath, come to that.

45

Apparently our contracts stipulate we appear in the series finale. Revolution
versus resolution. Character our current obsession. How our conflicts
define us. Contradiction *is* mother's milk. Only connect!
Only the gestures remain. First tragedy, then farce. Like family:
hard to get rid of, impossible to talk to. Like when the author
addresses us over the heads of her characters, diddling our plentitudes.
Sound a trifle twee? Surely. A bit precious? Your guess. As a means
of introducing a flake of pigment into this ongoing crisis of authenticity
we're thinking of trying out for a threesome. Desperate times, etc.
Might you assist *moi* in drafting the letter of intent?

46

Last night a few of the chulas from *Girls Gone Wild* dropped by
to discuss Heidegger. They get being but are having the devil's own time
with time. Occupational hazard, like the fact that they can't stop dancing.
Even when they pass out in one another's arms, when they're *Girls Gone
Blotto*, when their baby faces start surfacing like bodies after
a week at the bottom of the ole swimming hole way back when. But
they bring their own liquor and never leave without organizing
some form of bejesus, mostly involving lifting their arms
over their heads and pouring beer down the front of t-shirts spun from
fabric so fine that, just for shits and giggles, storybook princesses
use it for toilet paper. Have it shipped to Ever After
by the ton.

47

Our methods obscure, even to us. Especially to us. Yes,
when it comes to our methods, we prefer to be the last to know.
The lengths we're willing to go to protect the delicate
mechano-receptors of our ignorance are lengthy. For example,
vows and recipes must be written on any unavailable surface, even air.
Especially on air.

48

It's a fact that all discourses either model or mirror a subject.
It is also a fact that there are no facts. Is it a fact
that Friedrich famously averred there are no facts? Fact:
in the discourse of snow, *self* and *time* are interchangeable.
Fact: the closest term in snow for *death* is *landscape*.
Fact: snow is a religion in which the sun and things
that come in sixes abide deeply, deeply, deeply. Want more?
Snowmen are born showmen made in the image of their creator
and a woman isn't truly naked until some punctum pierces.
One little ribbon, some hair out of place. Children
of either sex instructed on estate planning by snowmen
who use hats and/or scarves as visual aids. Lastly, snowwomen
are taboo because a) breasts and b) they're lodestones
for Abomindable Snowmen which have been a fact of life
in the West since 1921.

49

Surfing the dialect is no substitute for apodicticity. Even
your dickless wonder in a bad haircut knows. Even ghosts,
living the heartbreak of severe repetition compulsion.
The way forward, brohanski, is into the past. We're talking
nonsynchronous form, as in our celebrated eight-minute short
of a man eating his own baby shoes. Or
what have you. The problem is memory. Or
lack of it. And both. Do you remember liberty,
equality, fraternity? The Four Horsemen
of Notre Dame? The trick is determining where
on the imploded pitch of postmodernism to pitch
your departure point. Right. Off you go.
23 skidoo.

50

Your frustration is completely understandable; i.e., beside the point.
So let us speak of the river. Grandma's hands. Worm-ridden stars. Write
what you know may be the worst advice ever given a tourist.
If the image evokes for the filmmaker a world that is largely missing,
in the spectator it induces endless extrapolations from what is actually seen.
What's a heartbreaking subjective correlative for suspension of disbelief?
Has your past proved the inexhaustible future the brochures promised?
For those of you following along at home, the better half of this week's simile
is *coral*. Prose was by this morning; the hell-bent dogs of syntax
circling the cabana. And where would we be without the subjunctive?
On the beach, under a velocirapturous sun, a woman out of myth anoints
her belly with oil. A return to form. And you with your pith hat and
spasmotics, stepping up, closing in: signifier without a signified.
If you ask her the time, her mind will race. Briefly. One billion
years ago, even before afternoons, this ocean under an ocean.
Our gift for castles in the troposphere, this abundant and richly-
figured creation, among our most cherished illusions. Even so,
make us an offer.

51

The poems on this side of the book would like it known they
have a complicated relationship with the poems opposite.

Right now in a street of Dongguan, China, a old woman squats
beside a wooden cage holding five ducks, three she owns outright,
and two she'll sell for a small commission. Rain, warm as flesh, is falling.

No one in her field of vision interests her as much as the pain in her shoulder.
In her mind, that pain is a flower, and each contraction of her heart infuses
that red flower with indigo, accents of which fade in the interval
between beats.

Between you and that woman yawns a gulf. Now
colour that gulf bone white, insert a dark, perfectly-straight,
needle-width perpendicular in the middle, graced on either side
with the soft ribs, the imperceptible transitions, of *sfumato*.

Now listen to the ducks. Now listen to this poem.

52

Night shift on the terminal wing. Our chamber
awaits. Our pathetic excuse for a last pillow abides. The nurses
adjust their bra straps, delve through training inches thick.
Metastasizing black windows. Down in the engine room
next to the morgue (where the real action is) a fresh dirigible
of wasted breath manhandled into the system. Meantime,
adjusting the wilt of our buttonhole, we abide, taking
our own sweet time.

53

When Death steps out on the town, fashion choice essentially
comes down to two options: monk's cowl and business casual.

The last time we saw Death, he was on a barstool
boring the daylights out of an off-duty nurse who saw it coming
from a very long way off.

The idea that Death would rather take you on in chess,
a rule-bound game you're pretty good at (if you do say so
yourself), rather than continue operations in a rule-free zone
in which he's effectively the only player in uniform,
would make an interesting premise for a foreign film.

You do know that Death is the photo bomber
in every selfie ever taken?

On the rare occasion Death takes the form of a woman
it invariably involves a lot of noirish lighting and lipstick. This is because
sex and death came up through the ranks together. And also because,
for a lot of men, a man dressed as a sexy woman
with definite designs on them is its own
special kind of horror.

54

Has it come to this? This? What's this? Weather
continues definite. Shall we describe it to you? *Fulsome* isn't
the word you took it for. What we love about it is how adept
its inscapes. And how timeless the blush flushing a virgin's
inbox. Lightly seasoned with last night's duende. Our descriptions
so mean a substitute for the real thing. O how often have we
decried the tantamount, the nearly vascular layering? In the capital,
synecdoche elevated to capital offense. Spiked heads
embellish the city gates, schlepping the death vowel. A few nobs
corner the market in fortune cookies and the next thing you know
(hint: below the limen is where it's always been). We saw your *grand recits*
in the arena. They didn't die well. So we've put together a selection
of artifacts from which entire lost civilizations might safely be inferred.
Under Augustus, the art of portraiture made a sharp turn to the right.
This is generally accepted. So put your money away. The next round
definitely on us.

55

We picked up two hitchhikers trying to get back
to the Real. The boy a dead loss but the girl a source. We liked
the way she looked out the window when the questions
got flocculent. At the smear of the passing hoo-ha. Like
she was thinking maybe we were a mistake she'd already
come to regret. In a very real sense, we were driving her to regret.
But regret, like the song says, is like the song says. On the other hand,
the boy's dirty fingernails generated their own gravitational field.
The end.

ACKNOWLEDGEMENTS

I wish to acknowledge everyone and everything that contributed to this book, but most of it now escapes me. There's the world, of course, and my wife, Judith (whose office happily rhymes with "life"), and my redoubtable editor and literary conscience, Carmine.

And then there are family and friends, near and departed, together with all the sly and semi-strange who've parked, howsoever briefly, in my demesne. You know who you are. And if you don't, shame on you.

Signal
EDITIONS

Carmine Starnino, Editor
Michael Harris, Founding Editor